"YUP . . . NOPE"

& Other Vermont Dialogues

D1571662

"YUP . . . NOPE"

& Other Vermont Dialogues

Arranged by Keith Jennison

Photographs by Neil Rappaport

The Countryman Press, Taftsville, Vermont 05073

ISBN 0-914378-14-7

Design and composition by Ian Wark,
VERMONT TYPEMASTERS, Fair Haven, Vt.

Printed in the United States of America
by SHARP OFFSET PRINTING INC., Rutland, Vt.

FOR PETER, MY BROTHER IN MORE THAN NAME

PHOTOGRAPHER'S NOTE

Most of the photographs were made in and around Pawlet, Vt. Many are fragments of intensive studies of local human environments. These places include a slate quarry, an old rascal's home, a store, a garage, a farm and the corner in North Pawlet where we live.

The spirit of the images is well contained in words of the poet William Carlos Williams: "One does not have to be uninformed to consort with cows...the local is the only thing that is universal."

———————

Much of my work has been supported by grants from the Vermont Council on the Arts and from faculty grants of Bennington College. I would also like to thank Elizabeth K. Dollard for her support when my work was just beginning.

NR

EDITOR'S NOTE

Many of the dialogues that appear in this book have
been included in other books. Some of them I used
myself in NEW HAMPSHIRE, published in 1944.
Attitudes and language don't change rapidly in
what, combining Vermont and New Hampshire,
Ralph Nading Hill aptly termed YANKEE KINGDOM.
To any reader who thinks that I am uncertain about
the difference between the two States, I can say only
that for a good many years a lot of other people were
too.

KWJ

1

''Do you know where William Gay lives?''

''Yup.''

''Mind telling us where?''

''Nope.''

''Well...where does he live?''

''Top of the hill over there.''

"You don't happen to know if he is at home or not, do you?"

"Nope. He ain't to home. What did you want with him?"

"We're the people who bought the Ransom place. Somebody told us Mister Gay might want to rent our pasture."

"I be he."

2

Grandfather ain't feeling as chipper as he did
thirty years ago...

he says he's starting to think maybe farming don't agree with him.

3

"Got any maple syrup for sale?"

"Nope."

"Man up the road told us you did have."

"He talks too much."

4

"What do you suppose they'll do when old man Appleby dies?"

"Likely they'll bury him."

5

"Think it's ever going to stop snowing?"

"It always has."

6

"Is there a criminal lawyer in this town?"

''We think so, but we haven't been able to prove it on him.''

7

"This farm must be doing pretty well if you can afford to pay a hired man."

''The hired man don't get paid. He works for me until his back pay amounts to the worth of the place..

then I go to work for him.''

8

A lady came into the store and asked: "Have you any Herbal Essence shampoo?"

"Nope."

"What about Shampoo with Egg?"

"Nope."

"Cashmere Bouquet soap?"

"Nope."

"Lovin' Spoonfuls cat food?"

"Nope. Them neither."

''This certainly isn't much of a store. I can't imagine what made me stop here. Now I guess I'll have to go all the way to Rutland.''

"We wouldn't have missed her none."

9

"We used to sit closer'n this when we first started going out together, Edward."

I'M PROUD TO BE A FARMER

DRINK MORE MILK

SEE VERMONT 75
D·3944

"I ain't moved."

10

"That Poultney road sign back at the corner is pointing in the wrong direction, isn't it?"

"Sure it is. But any damn fool knows how to get to Poultney."

11

"With all them candidates running, Les, why are you going to vote for Herb Mayberry?"

"He's the only one I ain't seen."

12

"My goodness, you folks up here in the hills certainly
are lost, aren't you?"

"Being lost ain't bad. It's getting found that bothers us."

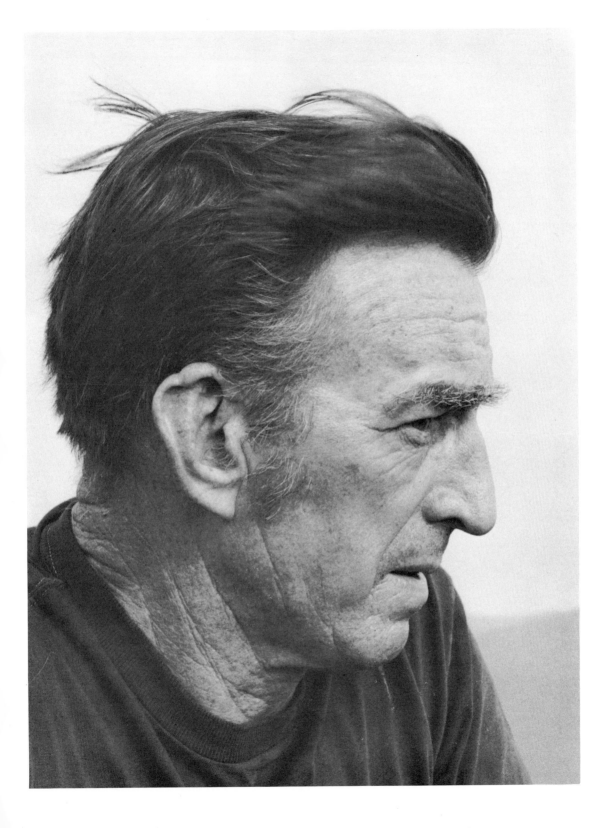

13

My little brother helped us with the freshening...

when it was all over, only thing he said was...

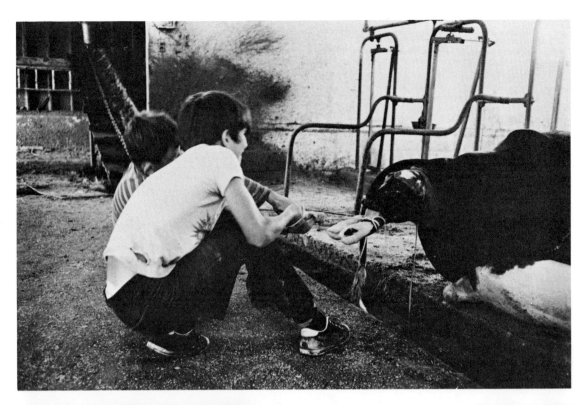

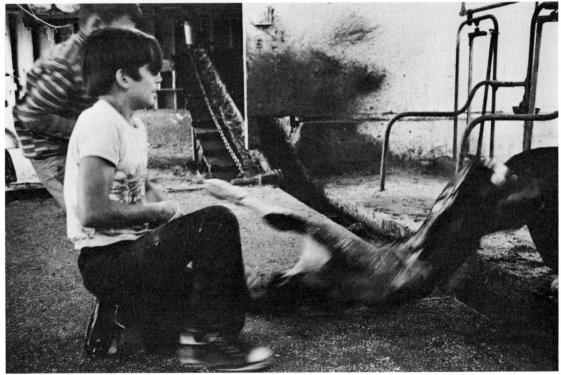

he didn't see how the calf got in there to begin with.

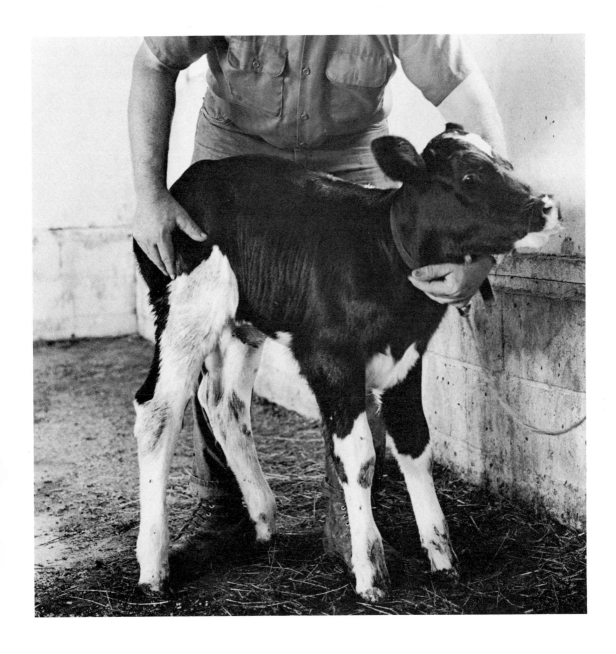

14

"The next train for Boston?"

"It left more'n five years ago."

15

''I guess I ain't got a lot longer to live and I ain't worried...

but it sure concentrates the mind.''

16

Old Robert J. once hired a Pennsylvania slate crew.

At the end of the day he compared their output to ours.

He walked over to their shanty and said: ''Well, boys I see you didn't hardly get into the race today.''

17

''How do you like the folks that came to live down the road last year?''

'Ain't found out yet. They don't neighbor none.''

18

Every man loves his native state,

whether he was born there or not.